ELEVATOR DOWN

THE SELLING OF A NATION

They Promised Us the Moon
Volume I

BY

WILLIAM PARKER ARCHIBALD

ELEVATOR DOWN
They Promised Us the Moon– Volume I

Copyright © 2015 by William Parker Archibald

Textual Advisement: Elaine Bush
Technical Support: Digital Depot (Maurice Tift)
Editing: Kit Duncan
Book Layout: Nat Mara

*A writer should struggle with the words
so the reader won't have to.*

– the author

When I was a youngster,

My father's favorite joke was about the farmer who had a pig with a wooden leg. When asked about it, the farmer went on for days about the virtues of the pig and how attached the family had become to it.

Acknowledging all of that, the visitor asked yet again why the animal had a wooden leg. To which the farmer responded, "Well, if you had a pig like that, would you eat it all at once?"

This, in a real way, is the story of America. I'm not questioning our love for it. That is well established. Rather, I'm questioning why, after centuries of toil and sacrifice, we've all of a sudden turned on it and are now devouring it with the reckless abandon of fools who sat down to feast on the goose that laid the golden egg.

Dedication

This book, indeed this whole endeavor to preserve, protect and defend that which has been given to us at such enormous cost, is dedicated to all of the patriots, both living and dead and to my good friend and mentor,

Millard Fuller,
founder of Habitat for Humanity International and the Fuller Center for Housing.

ELEVATOR

DOWN

1969 To the Present

There's no way that life should be this hard, not in this land, not in this time. At the end of the 1960's, beginning of the 1970's, this country was on top of the heap with no one remotely within striking distance. Oh sure, the Cold War was still raging, but we had touched down on the Moon just as communist Russia, crumbling under the weight of its own broken promises, was beginning its slow, downward spiral toward certain doom. Within two brief decades, once proud Soviet coal miners would be striking for something as basic as bar soap while people stood in endless lines for the few pieces of rotten produce on their grocers' shelves.

Americans, on the other hand, had good jobs, career positions with solid benefits and pensions. One person on a blue collar wage could feed an entire family, put the kids through college, own their home outright and retire young enough to travel the country in an RV. There was pride, there was hope, there was every expectation that the future would be even rosier and life all the easier. Why wouldn't it be? After all, they promised us the Moon.

Now look at us. If we haven't lost our job or home, or had our savings and hope of retiring wiped out, we know someone in our family or down the street that has. Just this week, I found a person living in his car at an interstate highway rest area. Friends and I are now scrambling to get him on his feet. This situation was simply unimaginable but a brief time ago.

Two Seminal Events

Two seminal events occurred. The first took place on July 21, 1969, when, in my opinion, America reached the apex of its ascendance by trouncing the Russians through winning the "space race." We were the first to make a manned lunar landing before returning safely home to planet Earth.

The second occurred just three years later in 1972, when Richard Nixon, aka "Tricky Dicky," in what the press dubbed his "greatest diplomatic achievement," opened the doors for trade with mysterious and secretive China.

The backdrop for this historic event was a much touted ping pong match between China's best players and ours. We may no longer remember who won that contest, but when we skip ahead to my local newspaper in August of 2011, it becomes clear that we lost far more than a game.

What, pray tell, was the big news in Americus, Georgia, that caught not only my eye but also the attention of NBC, CNN and *The Today Show*? It was only that China's ever increasing trade imbalance with the US now had a counterbalance. That's right, we finally had something they wanted and needed. You guessed it, chopsticks. China apparently has a shortage of lumber, so they started manufacturing them here in the USA.

The newspaper interviewed workers at the new Americus, Georgia, facility where I live. Virtually all of them stated how relieved they were to finally have a job, any job, in a community with shuttered factories and a 14% unemployment rate. They also repeatedly said that they saw this new plant as a definite step in the right direction. One televised version of the same event went even further. They added an important bit of information overlooked by my paper and most Americans.

While we were busy filling boxes with chopsticks for export to China, the Chinese exported something to us as well. It arrived in slightly larger containers.

They sent us a brand new Oakland Bay Bridge. That's right, the whole thing, stretching from one shore clear over to the other. It seems that California, with its record unemployment, saw fit to forego hiring its own people and decided instead to save money by purchasing an entire bridge from China. It consisted of nine segments spanning from Oakland to San Francisco.

In just a little over forty years, the United States has gone from being one of the wealthiest countries in the world to one of the most deeply indebted, while China, during the same period of time, rose from rice paddies to the world's largest exporter of consumer goods.

The History

What many of us forget is that when western television crews first went into China, the West was literally holding its breath, fearing the first images to beam back home to America would be those of people starving in the streets. That's how poor they were. They had nothing. They were penniless and little better off than the people of North Korea today. Their country had no rich mineral deposits, no silver and gold, nor any intellectual property worth marketing. They had nothing at all, just billions of people living a subsistence life under communism.

The obvious question is, what did they have that we wanted? The answer is sheer numbers. We didn't look at China as having the things we wanted. We looked at China as having the consumers we wanted. Coca Cola executives, to mention just one interest, were drooling over the prospect of having billions of people drinking Coke. After all, the American business model is simple: create a desire, then stoke the fire.

The problem was that a soft drink was ridiculously out of reach for the typical Chinese peasant – and that's what most of them were at that time, peasants living off the land. Undeterred, American corporations set up state-of-the-art factories that gave Chinese workers the money to purchase Coca Colas and other American goods. At the same time, this provided a vastly cheaper way for these corporations to make things, thanks to a much lower pay scale in China. These same products would then be shipped stateside where they clobbered competitors who still paid wages commensurate with supporting a typical American family. In response, companies back home, desiring to remain competitive in this new cost cutting environment, followed suit, shuttered their factories and joined the mad dash overseas.

To Recap

There we have it. We were riding high as a nation, but the captains of industry weren't satisfied. They wanted more, more profits and more money. The only way they could do it was to increase market share by selling us down the river. So what if Americans lost their jobs? They didn't care. They were putting money into the pockets of a new pool of potential consumers who would then, for the very first time, be able to buy their goods.

To sweeten the deal even more, these same captains of industry then turned around and made a dollar off the very economy they were destroying. Once proud American workers, now with less disposable income as all of the good (and even poor paying) jobs were fast disappearing, had little choice but to gobble down these cheap goods that began to pour into this country. In short, the greed of the few set off a chain of events that has bankrupted us as a nation and left us struggling at the very time we should be reaping the harvest of all those who worked so hard and sacrificed so much.

A Cancerous Growth

On the surface, it looked like growth and in a certain sense it was. Yet, it was a destructive growth, an out of control cancer, a ballooning tumor destroying everything in its path. Wal-Mart is a prime example of this dynamic. Yes, it shot up fast and grew like a weed, but it single handedly wiped out most small town business districts across the country, leaving them boarded up and desolate. High quality family run businesses where people were welcomed with a sincere, "How may I help you?" were replaced with impersonal big box stores employing disinterested greeters who were clueless about the thousands of square feet of low-end merchandise behind them. For the first time in America's history, the race wasn't to the top, but rather to the lowest level.

People were retooling their thinking away from asking how to better their position through innovation and improvement to the more insidious question of how to improve their position by getting their neighbor to surrender more and more. If the item or service cost X number of dollars, our question became the same as that asked by Wal-Mart, "Can you do it for less?"

Colonialism

When a developed world power, such as Great Britain, establishes a relationship of economic dominance over an undeveloped land, such as it did with the thirteen American colonies, it is called colonialism. Its intention is not to advance the weaker state, but rather to exploit it for its own benefit. It does this by dismantling or preventing the development of manufacturing facilities in the fledgling nation. This forces the weaker country to sell its raw materials to the dominant country (as it has nothing else to export). The proceeds from the sale of these raw materials are then used to purchase finished goods from the dominant country. This bleeds wealth from the weaker state and, in time, demoralizes its people as sooner or later they come to realize they have no hope for real advancement. Rather, they are trapped in a seemingly endless cycle of supplying both raw materials and a steady stream of customers to the very nation that has them in its grip.

Reverse Colonialism

In the forty plus years since opening the doors of trade with China, we in the US have witnessed, and indeed facilitated, a complete reversal of the above dynamic. For instead of creating more production jobs here and a global customer base to buy our goods, we have done just the opposite. We have laid off our own workforce, carted up the very machinery they were using, shipped it overseas and have become consumers of the goods we previously made here at home. Then, we find ourselves scratching our heads and wondering why we have shuttered factories, record unemployment and staggering trade deficits. It isn't rocket science, folks. The reason we have fewer jobs here is because we bundled them up with nice little ribbons and shipped them all overseas to China.

Now, the American worker is on the sidelines, watching economic reports on the news that no longer impact him or her. For even when recessions end and things do improve on Wall Street, the good news has little bearing on things here at home as the country is experiencing what the press has dubbed a "jobless recovery."

This means, as the label suggests, that even though demand is up and American corporations are turning in record profits, they aren't hiring people here at home, but rather they are hiring foreigners to work in facilities they have built overseas.

Reasons for Sending Factories to China

I. *We honestly believed we could do without them.* It was as though we bought into the notion that if we moved money around fast enough, it would somehow create sufficient inertia to keep the wind in our sails. Reality has proven this simply isn't the case. No matter how many times a slick bank ad refers to some new line of credit as a "product," the truth of the matter is that money is not and never has been a product. It is nothing more and nothing less than a marker for, or representative of, tangible goods and services. Money doesn't make money. People make the goods and produce the services that are measured in terms of dollars and cents.

II. *Arrogance. We thought "menial work" was beneath us.* If we had to produce anything, it would be high tech items like computer chips, jet engines or advanced medical imaging equipment. Unskilled labor in poorer nations would make mundane things like frying pans and dust mops. We would devote ourselves to the high end gadgetry that made the Silicon Valley famous.

(Obviously, this wasn't such a great idea.)

The problem, of course, is that electronics make up only a sliver of our Gross National Product (the sum total of all we produce). The lion's share consists of everyday things like bath towels, vacuum cleaners, ball point pens, and electrical outlet covers. These are what make or break an economy. Today, all of these items bear the label "Made in China" and increasingly, the high tech items do as well.

III. *Good Old Garden Variety Greed: "Let's get rich by making things cheaper in China!"* Out of a desire to make a quick buck, companies began producing items in China for less than 50 cents on the dollar and then transported them here for sale. Even after the cost of shipping them halfway around the world, they still enjoyed a much bigger profit than if they paid workers here to produce them. What they didn't figure was that in time, American wallets would run out of money to buy ironing boards as more and more of us got laid off. And now, while our economy is shrinking, China is enjoying record expansion. They not only profit from selling us all of those ironing boards that we previously made here, they also make interest on loans we've taken out to cover the lack of income we've suffered since laying ourselves off. It's beyond ludicrous. It's insane.

Thanks for your "New World Order" George (Bush I), but take it back; we're no longer going to fall for it!

Unless one's country is terribly small, like Monaco, or an island nation like Bermuda, most items for sale are generally produced right there in the home country by the citizens who use them. This only makes sense as it provides jobs and a stable base to the economy.

Yet, while most nations have been building up their industrial base, we've had the "New World Order" shoved down our throats by President after President from both parties. How's that been working out for us? Apparently, it's not been going too well. We've been in decline for decades. We've been able to mask it by first working more hours on the job, then taking on more jobs, then sending out more people from our households to do more work, but we still fall farther and farther behind.

The Myth Was That Globalization Would Increase Sales

In reality, other nations were already foaming at the mouth, saving every dime they could muster, just to purchase these very things that at one time were only produced here. Now, the very same inventions that were previously American-made are no longer headed for the docks of Oakland, California, Seattle, Washington, or Baltimore, Maryland, but rather to far off ports of call. We've turned the whole thing backwards. Computers and other high end products are now made overseas.

It's A Global Financial Shift, Not a Meltdown

When Democrats stick their heads out of the hole we've all dug together, they immediately notice a lack of jobs and incorrectly correlate it to the Great Depression. This is a really big, huge, gargantuan, monumental, running out of sufficient words to describe it, mistake. Why? Because, comparing what's going on to the1930's sets up a whole series of incorrect assumptions that lead to prescribing the wrong medicine.

To begin with, unlike the 1930's, this is not and never has been bad news for everyone. China and India are doing quite well, thank you. In fact, they are on an upward trajectory every bit as pronounced as the downward trend we're experiencing here. It's as though we're all on a great big economic teeter-totter and they are on the other end, going up just as we are coming down.

It's No Coincidence - Their Rise Is Linked To Our Decline

How could it be otherwise? We've given them everything they need to flourish, while at the same time, we've taken away all that has supported and protected us. For starters, we have handed over our advanced technology, not only in blueprints, but often in real time production capabilities as we sent the actual machines American workers were using to make our industries purr. Then, we took down reasonable trade barriers (that up until now have kept our wages and standard of living high), while at the same time giving competitors our "most favored nation status." This gives them an unfair advantage over the few American owned and operated factories that still remain. Then, to come full circle and complete the process, we have provided a steady stream of customers to buy their goods.

The second mistake that flows from correlating today's situation to a scaled back version of the Great Depression (where we assume the whole world is suffering – which again, isn't true) is to assume that only the government has deep enough pockets to stimulate growth by hiring people. This all sounds plausible, but none of it is accurate. The treasury might have deep pockets, but there are only holes in them. Not only doesn't the government have any money, it has also just about reached its credit limit.

The Democrats' Flawed Response

Due to the Democrats incorrectly assessing today's predicament, their attempts at getting things back on track are marginally successful at best. They're a bit like a family with an unemployed head of the household and a college age son who can't find a summer job. Just as they are pondering the poor job market, they wake up to the fact that their house desperately needs a fresh coat of paint. When they put the two realities together, it only seems logical to go to the bank, take out a home equity loan and hire their teenager to do the painting. This way the son gets a summer job and money for school and the house gets a much needed facelift.

On the surface this may appear prudent, but it really only worsens their plight. For the son's increase in income is one and the same as the family's increase in indebtedness. In fact, it is even worse than a simple transfer of funds from one pocket to another. For the family is now not only out the money they have paid their son, they also have to pay back the interest on the bank loan, bear the cost of the paint and pay higher interest rates on future loans. That is, if they can obtain them, as this increased debt load makes them a riskier loan prospect.

What the family needs is real income from an outside source. An example of this, using our illustration again, would be the son getting a job producing something. Then the money in his pocket would be coming from someplace other than the family's own checking account. In so doing, he'd actually participate in the laws of supply and demand. He'd be providing something (supply) to meet the needs of a customer (demand) who is able to pay for it. This results in wealth accumulation for the family.

The Republicans' Flawed Response

When Republicans pull their heads out of the same hole we've all dug together, they come up with a completely different and equally impoverishing idea for solving it. As strict believers in free markets, they'd have us go toe-to-toe with the third world countries that now compete for the jobs we sent overseas.

They look around and see that many competing countries don't have a minimum wage, so they attempt to freeze increases on ours or do away with it altogether. They also notice other nations cut costs by ignoring pollution and safety standards that we take for granted in the US. Again, out of a desire to be competitive, they seek to relax or do away with regulations we have in place here.

The question is, do we really want to do whatever it takes to compete with populations that have no labor laws, no safety or environmental standards and would be thrilled to earn a mere $700 a year? If we do win, at what cost do we win? Under these circumstances, is not winning the same as surrendering the high standard of living our parents and grandparents fought so hard to create? We're already seeing that for many, the minimum wage has become the maximum wage, and what was once a rock bottom floor has become a new ceiling. Americans now have to work longer and harder, not at one, but two or three jobs just to pay the same bills that one paycheck used to cover. As time moves on, fewer and fewer good jobs are available anywhere for anyone. It's not just the assembly line worker who is out of work, now it's also the car dealer and cabinet maker who no longer have the funds to be cash paying customers themselves as they no longer have the assembly line workers to purchase their goods. It's the police officers and school teachers in municipalities who no longer have the tax revenues to support them, and church pastors and chaplains, like me, who find church budgets shrinking.

Please Note: *Just as one good rain is not the end of a drought, so, too, even if there is an economic upswing, it doesn't change the fact that America is hemorrhaging money.*

New World Order Created by Republicans and Democrats

Each proposed response to our already bleak economy, from both the Democrats and Republicans, is scary enough when taken individually, but when put together, we have the true horror that is unfolding right before our very eyes. When adjusted for inflation, we are actually earning far less than our parents did (thanks to the Republican disdain for both collective bargaining and hiking the minimum wage). Then, to cover the shortfall that is created when lower wages bring in reduced tax revenues, we borrow more and more from China, the very nation that has us by the throat.

Put the two together and the Republicans have us work harder for less income and the Democrats borrowing more to make up the difference. One feeds into the other and worsens the whole. The longer this goes on and the deeper we sink, the better it is for China. For we are no longer merely consumers of their goods. They use the profit they make from us to loan us the money we need in order to cover the shortfall of revenue we're losing to them. We're increasingly like coal miners shopping at the company store. The question is, "At what point will we no longer be able to fund the interest on the debt, let alone pay off the principle?"

Enter the Wisdom of Roe Nelson

This whole mess could have been avoided if we all grew up, as I did, across the street from the Nelsons on Colston Drive in Chevy Chase, Maryland. They were faithful members of St. Paul Methodist Church where my father was the pastor.

When I was an enterprising young man of eleven, I walked across the street and asked Mrs. Nelson if I could mow her lawn. My sales pitch was simple. I'd cut the whole thing, the front and back yard, for only 50 cents. The words were barely out of my mouth before she replied, "Yeah, but what about David? He has a family to feed?"

With that my heart sank, not because I didn't get the job, but because I immediately knew, even at the age of eleven, that I had missed the mark and failed morally. She was right. What about David? David was the swellest guy (eleven year old terminology) I'd ever met. He was a kind, elderly man who drove his rickety truck out to the burbs every week only to have us kids swear, in all sincerity, that our dogs would never bite him despite the fact that they never stopped nipping at his heels.

David didn't merely mow lawns, he manicured them. He worked and worked, trimmed and trimmed until every three bedroom home looked like a regal estate. He earned a lot more than the $6.00 he charged the Nelsons (good money in 1966 dollars.) He earned the highest respect of everyone he met. I'd only be too proud to become a man like David. The question remains, "What about David?" He had expenses beyond my nickel ice cream cones and 50 cent movie tickets. He had a wife, probably house payments and grand-kids. While I'd be thrilled to live on a mere fraction of his paycheck, there was no way in the world that he could lower his rates sufficiently to compete with me.

If we translate this to global economics, we'd easily equate American workers today with David. They didn't just happen upon their standard of living, they earned it. On the basis of their efforts, they have assumed lifelong responsibilities they can't and shouldn't easily put aside. To pull the rug out from under them by handing their livelihoods over to people living in a totally foreign economy that requires infinitely less and to do it all in the name of "fair" trade is an assault on everything I know to be good and decent and true. Yet it is exactly what has happened to Davids all over this great country.

Can We Get It For Less?

In the late 1990s, I was a pastor who met with a committee responsible for hiring a new church secretary. We had managed to find the perfect candidate, a woman who is still there to this day. To my amazement and deep dissatisfaction, the question the panel asked wasn't, "What's the most we can offer her?" Rather, it was, "What's the least we can offer without losing her?" This was a church committee! I was so beside myself that when we finally did hire her, I immediately sought her out, apologized for the pittance we were paying and told her that henceforth this congregation wouldn't be singing *They Will Know We Are Christians By Our Love* until the church earned the right to do so.

When It Comes to Economics
The Circle Will Truly Be Unbroken!

What am I missing here? This a democratic country where each time we offer to employ someone, be it a babysitter or corporate executive, we have the right to be either good, loving and decent, or we can selfishly nickel and dime each person like a bunch of Ebenezer Scrooges. The economy will continue either way, but I offer all of us this fair warning. When it comes to finances, the circle will definitely be unbroken. The same tide that goes out eventually comes back in. There are no supernatural, beyond our control, don't know what we can do about it, mysterious "market forces at work" here. It's only us. We are the ones who hire, fire and set the wages.

Sooner or later, the amount we give out to others as employers will be the same feast or famine that is available when it is our turn to sit at the table. The dollars that leave our hands when we employ someone are the same dollars that are drawn upon when we ourselves seek a fair, livable wage as a worker. Put a lot in and get a lot out. Put in a morsel, and we'll all barely scrape by like dogs under their master's table. We can create a nation of well-paying jobs, or we can continue to take on the role of paupers. It's up to us, for ultimately, we are in fact our "brother's keeper."

Of Fire and Water

I'd like to offer a few brief observations about money. First, the scout in me tells me building a sound economy is best likened to building a roaring fire. When good, honorable wages are given in exchange for good, honorable work, it is akin to putting logs at the base. For the working class, unlike the wealthy, cannot afford to sideline their money. They spend it almost as quickly as it comes in. This provides a constant source of fuel that heats up the entire economy from the bottom to the top.

The other image that comes to mind is water. Water, by nature, naturally flows to the lowest point available. When a fabulously wealthy economy at the top of its game is put right next to the poorest economy at the bottom (for that's where the US and China were in 1972), and all of the barriers between them are removed, it's only obvious and natural that two things are going to happen. First, the levels in China are going to rise and levels in America are going to fall. How could it be any other way? And, that is exactly what has happened. It only seems equally obvious to me that while we still have some water in our pool, we'd better stem the tide.

What about Wages and Inflation?

Having gone through years of self-inflicted poverty out of a deep seated desire to lend assistance to others, I know firsthand about "huffing it down the road" with only shoe leather to soften, if not the ride, then definitely the stride. While a marked improvement over going barefoot, shoe leather had its limitations. And so, in time, all that wishful thinking by many a walker about floating down the road on a cushion of air led to someone coming up with the idea of an inflatable tire. What's significant here is that a tire is, in a sense, a closed system or universe. It has to be this way in order to hold enough air together in a compressed state so as to raise it up to a new level, a level above the rest, a level that is so wonderful it is not only like, but actually is floating on air.

Now, Lord knows there is plenty of air outside the tire. It's all around, infinitely cheap and instantly available, but pity the fool that opens the valve trying to take advantage of it. All that happens is that the tire loses pressure and the whole thing goes flat, leaving one stranded as others race past.

I Fear We Are Like That Fool

Of course, wages are going to be lower outside our borders, in countries that are impoverished, but trying to take advantage of them is as foolish as trying to replace pressurized air with unpressurized air. It, too, will leave us deflated and parked by the curb. Right now, our tires are riding awfully low and we need to pump them up again. To do so is really quite simple. It's a two-step process. First, we need to apply patches where needed and seal up any leaks, and then pump up our standard of living by allowing wages to return to the levels they were at before we opened the valves.

We Mustn't Hinder the Natural Increase of Wages

We have been told over and over again that inflation is bad, that the government must stop it cold in its tracks whenever and wherever it rears its ugly head. The question is, where are these opportunities? We are led to believe that nothing can be done about the dramatic upswing in the cost OPEC charges for oil, even though they know they can always depend on us to send in troops to do their bidding when they get into trouble; and these wars aren't cheap. They drive inflation right through the roof.

We also know that drug companies, even those based in the US, get away with charging us more than anyone else in the world for the very medications they manufacture here. Why? It is simply because they can. In fact, Uncle Sam has flat out rejected using its position as the nation's largest health care consumer to negotiate lower drug costs on our behalf. And the list goes on and on and on. In fact, I can't think of too many prices or charges the government regulates, except for public utilities.

But when it is our turn to seek increases in our pay checks so that we might maintain buoyancy with these rising costs that threaten to drown us in red ink, watch out! Would-be watchdogs in Congress, who take pride in protecting us from rising inflation, jump up and pounce. "Inflationary," they cry as they rush in to freeze increases in our personal incomes.

When I was coming up in the 1950's and 60's, costs were going up, but wages were keeping pace with them. Inflation was there, but like grace that can always stretch just a little bit more to cover increases in sin, wages somehow always rose with them and we were OK. All of that changed when Ronald Reagan became President. The minimum wage became frozen and remained that way for years.

Now, in fairness to him, it is true that he entered office in a time of outrageous inflation and the brakes had to be put on whenever possible, but the problem was that those brakes were never released once the economy improved. From then on, other forms of wealth accumulation were allowed to increase, but wage increases were automatically deemed "inflationary" and curtailed.

We want to slow increases in everything except wages. For when costs remain the same and wages increase, our standard of living goes up...Think about it!

Where Was Our Government When We As Workers Needed Protection?

The problem is, Administration after Administration have sat by and passively watched as foreign companies, with the active support of their home governments, have practiced every trick in the book to gain market share. For the folks in Washington to be all laissez-faire fare and hands off while American workers were getting clobbered by these conspiratorial trade practices and then turn around and be on us like syrup on pancakes the few times we were able to catch a break and get a raise is the height of hypocrisy. It seems folks in Washington have forgotten that it is government "For the People."

The One-Two Punch to the American Standard of Living

The first blow came when Ronald Reagan did battle with unions that were a bit too greedy for their own good. Air traffic controllers went on strike and when they didn't meet his deadline for returning to work, they were summarily fired. Subsequent unions fell one by one, including Greyhound bus drivers who watched in horror as a fellow worker got run over by one of their own buses and subsequently died. This was soon followed by the squashing of any and all attempts to raise the minimum wage.

The second blow came from the Bushes' and Clintons' push for globalization. First, there was George Bush I's relentless call for a "New World Order" followed by Bill Clinton's push for the North American Free Trade Agreement (NAFTA). Together, they put downward pressure on wages as they expanded the pool of workers to include the entire globe. Whereas before Americans were only competing against each other for work, now, all of a sudden, they found themselves competing with workers around the world who could live on substantially less money in foreign countries.

From that point on, American workers didn't stand a chance. They had it coming from above and below. On the top side, they found it hard to get any increases in pay as the unions that kept pushing for higher and higher wages with better and better benefits were suddenly gone. On the low side, globalization meant employers could now reach across the oceans and get the same work done for a fraction of what they were previously paying workers here. The American Dream of making it big financially was now severely crippled and our lives have been forever changed.

The Difference Between Now and Then

A century earlier, the great robber barons of the Gilded Age, the likes of the Rockefellers and Carnegies, had also benefitted from cheap labor. They, too, had made their millions off of the backbreaking sweat of others. That wasn't new. It's as old as capitalism itself. The tradeoff back then was that even though the workers of that day didn't reap the full rewards to which they were entitled, their future descendants did. That was about to change.

What was new this time around was that American capitalists were no longer investing in America, but rather diverting funds from here to the industrialization and development of competing nations. It was no longer true that "What was good for GM was good for America." To the contrary, the exact opposite was often the case.

Undeterred, when we as consumers wanted more, we didn't look for raises. Rather, we kept going back again and again and breached the walls of our purposefully inflated, self-contained little economic bubble that we had been living in. This led to deflating our economic situation here while at the same time adding lift to competing economies.

Wages, like tires, do need to be inflated from time to time. It's true. Just try to drive a car or an economy where that hasn't been done in a few years and you'll know what I'm talking about.

A Long String of Presidents Have Presided Over the Great American Giveaway

All kinds of Presidential libraries can be built and all manner of foundations started to honor the memory of our eight past heads of state, but no amount of window dressing can cover the simple fact that this country has been in a persistent state of decline for decades. The facts speak for themselves.

On the watch of President after President, from both sides of the aisle, the United States has stumbled and stumbled badly. It has lost ground, thereby opening the door for lesser countries to rush in and gain political, economic, and industrial clout.

The ineptitude of these "leaders" has been striking. How else can we explain going from a safe cruising altitude to a precipitous nosedive in little more than a single generation? Opportunity after opportunity has been squandered time and time again. These lapses in judgment have been so severe that the common citizen cannot help but wonder just who side these "leaders" has been on. Did they actually think extending "most favored nation status" to another country meant favoring their interests above ours? Judging from their track record, it would seem they actually did, for in situation after situation, their decisions increased the standing of other nations while diminishing ours.

Let's be clear. The "Great American Giveaway" didn't start with China. It started much earlier than that with Japan. China has merely been following their playbook. Both countries lured us in with their cheap labor only to then systematically begin to take, take, take and take some more. They smiled and bowed to us as they toured our jet propulsion laboratories and manufacturing plants (all the while taking copious notes).

They studied at our best universities and made detailed blueprints of our most innovative products, then went home and set up state of the art factories to compete against us. And where were our nation's leaders? They were busy smiling and bowing right back at them.

Which President stood up when Japan dumped artificially cheap steal on Bethlehem, Pennsylvania, wiping out a proud industry and pillar of American strength? Not one of them.

Which President took decisive action when the Japanese government repeatedly usurped the concept of fair trade by actively doing whatever it took to defeat American competition one industry at a time? Again, not one of them rose to our defense. Reagan finally did step in to protect Harley Davidson, but that was the only company. The rest of our manufacturers were on their own, and as a result, a large number of them no longer exist or are greatly diminished.

President after President made sure we kept on the straight and narrow and played by the rules while at the same time doing nothing to stem the illicit practices aimed at our workers and the nation as a whole. This dynamic was reminiscent of US Olympic Teams competing before the fall of the communist bloc. Back then, our athletes, with little or no financial support, went up against East Germans who had been in government funded sports camps since childhood. To sweeten the deal even further, their coaches stepped in and doled out huge amounts of performance enhancing drugs and hormones so potent as to call into question the very gender of their female athletes.

When the Japanese took all of the money they had accrued from years of lopsided trading and set out to buy America, what Administration so much as raised a protest let alone acted to stop it? Not one of them. If it wasn't for a protracted slump in their economy, the Japanese would probably own enormous chunks of America by now including much of Manhattan just as they currently own much of Hawaii. So easily we forget that Reagan's first trip after leaving office was to fly directly to Japan to receive a check for 2 million dollars. What was the rationale for Japan paying him so much money?

It was supposedly for delivering a few speeches. Delivering a few speeches? Do the math. Ronald Reagan earned $400,000 a year. To earn $2,000,000 he would have had to work for five years as chief executive or "deliver a few speeches" in Japan so insignificant that none of us know hardly anything about them.

Look at the Japanese industrial market share before he took office and compare it to where it was after he left office. Then look at what happened to America's factories and our workforce during the same period. I'd say that Japan got an incredible deal for a mere $2 million.

Which President took steps to protect our technology from blatant theft by our competitors? Not one of them. Which President took steps to keep wages of the American worker high? Barack Obama, almost single handedly saved Detroit's auto industry and with it what little remains of our industrial complex, but for the most part, Chief Executive after Chief Executive have sat idly by and watched our standard of living plummet.

To top it off, American companies are saddled with an ever increasing barrage of rules and regulations that tip the scales even more in their competitors' favor. America is now one of the last places in the world where one would want to open a factory. We can't even speak to an American sales rep when we dial up an American corporation as a huge percentage of customer call centers are now located overseas in places like the Philippines and other foreign lands.

Presently, we export more empty boxes than products and borrow bazillions and bazillions of dollars every year, not to pay the principle, mind you, but rather just the interest on our ever growing loan to China. Why, pray tell, do we even have unemployment claims of American workers who can't find jobs here while we are buying things from the very same China that turns around and collects interest on the money we are borrowing to support our idled work force. It is absolutely ludicrous.

We may have the largest Navy in the world, but so what? We don't even control the western hemisphere anymore. China does by virtue of it turning the Monroe Doctrine on its head by buying control of the canal from corrupt Panamanian officials. Bill Clinton did nothing to stop it. Why didn't he intervene? It's because he took campaign contributions from China and therefore was obliged to keep his mouth shut when it happened.

Since then, there hasn't been so much as a verbal rebuke of either Panama or China regarding the sale, let alone a change in China's most favored nation status. To the contrary, with the ongoing silence of each successive Presidential Administration, China has become so secure in its new found home away from home that it is now working to dramatically increase the size of ships that can pass through under their watchful eye, as we sit back and get accustomed to our new role as mere spectators. As if this isn't bad enough, that same nation is now embarking on construction of a second wider canal.

It is beyond even Webster's definition of "pathetic." Here we are with our national leadership, acting like a bunch of deer in the headlights, passively watching ships go through what in effect has become China's canal. Worse yet, many of you readers are probably wondering by now, "Why all of the focus on China?" The answer is really quite simple. It's because no one else is raising any alarms.

The Chinese are like the student who arrived late and unprepared, yet had the good fortune to be befriended by a classmate who allowed the copying of answers that were obtained by the first student studying long and hard into the night.

I'm quite certain that instead of focusing on the boost the US gave China, there will be a backlash of scorn once we stem the flow; for by continually giving with no expectation of anything in return, we've created a sense of entitlement that can only lead to resentment once the well beaten path of a one sided relationship is no longer used.

As it is, we've given them cause to believe that if they continue to manipulate their currency to their unfair trade advantage, ignore our copyright laws, allow the pervasive pirating of our name brands and introduce, on occasion, dangerous toxins into products we consume our only response will be to send over a polite delegation to have a little chat. Of course, these conversations have never changed anything due to the simple fact that the Chinese aren't stupid.

Something tells me they aren't exactly trembling in their boots. They know that if they continue to ignore us, the worse that will happen is that we will send over yet another delegation with the fair warning that if things don't turn around quickly, we'll be back to speak with them yet again.

What Shall I Say To Those Who Have Gone On Before?

Those of you who are so casual and nonplused about surrendering our position of prominence, not to just any nation, but to one that has gobbled down whatever has been handed to them on a silver platter and stolen the rest...please tell me, what should I say to those who have gone before us when we meet on some ethereal shore and they inquire as to their beloved country? Should I tell them, who gave even when they had nothing left to give, that we just got bored with the blessings and opted to give them away? Is that what I should tell them?

And what, pray tell, should I say to the legions of brave souls, the likes of John Paul Jones, who, when asked if he was going to surrender, replied, "I have not yet begun to fight!" or to the farm boys of Pennsylvania and Delaware whose frozen feet bled in the snow at Valley Forge? Do I tell them that we felt it was inevitable that another country would overtake us and, therefore, put up not the slightest resistance?

And what, may I ask, do I say to those whose bodies are still trapped beneath the decks of the Battleship

Arizona or are buried in Flanders Fields when they ask about their nation and its place in the world? Do I tell them that we surrendered it to not just any nation, but to a nation that kills prisoners in order to sell their organs to the highest bidder and forces couples who conceive more than one child to have an abortion even if it is against their will? Is that the message you want to give these brave builders of our republic? That we just assumed our time was over because the television commentators kept saying over and over again that all empires rise only to fall and our time had run its course? No, I won't be telling them any such thing. You'll have to share the news. For I have neither the heart nor the stomach to convey such sadness.

Hello?
Where In The World
Have Our "Leaders" Been?
What Have They Been Doing?

Name the government official, from any party or branch of our government, who has raised holy havoc over China's repeated attempts at hacking into our national security computers. There aren't any such voices, at least at high enough levels of power to be heard, that have stood up and said, "Stop!" Name the official, from either party, who has told China that Antarctica belongs to everyone, so come back, pick up the flag you planted on the bottom of the ocean floor and please don't upset the tranquility of the place by trying another stunt like that again. Name the American President, Republican or Democrat, who has stood up to China's clear acts of aggression and called a spade a spade. There aren't any. Why not?

China Has Been Waging A Cyber and/or Trade War And We Respond As If To An Isolated Crime Here And There. Why?

To classify these provocative actions as mere "cybercrimes" is a gross mischaracterization of the seriousness of these aggressive acts. To under respond only encourages more incursions as it conveys weakness or worse yet, a total indifference on our part.

No One in Washington Seems Too Awfully Concerned

For over forty years, we have extended China our "most favored nation" trade status and put up with their trade policies that are clearly designed to siphon wealth from our nation and send it to theirs. Yet, no one has put up the warning flags let alone called for action. To the contrary, Administration after Administration, from Nixon to the present, have bent over backwards to accommodate China's gorilla-like trade practices that have robbed us blind, while at the same time, holding budget talks on cutting services here at home.

Globalization Leads to Individual Disempowerment

While it may feel wise to bring all of the world's people under one global umbrella as the larger the political entity the fewer the borders that foster conflict and division, in reality, it diminishes the goal of equal representation. For the larger the crowd, the harder it is to have individual voices heard and the more tempting it is for power mongers to seek dominance. Democracies function best when people have a sense of ownership and rightfully believe that their individual input matters.

That is why we have municipal and county governments, then state governments, and finally the national or federal government. If we want to change something on the local level, we, as individuals, can deal with it on the local level where a lone voice is most powerful. The larger the issue, the more people are needed to bring attention to it. In this way, the system retains proportionality. One person can be heard on things that affect him or her directly, but they need the support of the masses to affect change on issues that impact the whole.

To keep our country spinning like a top
we must remember:

It Can
Be Rightfully
Said That Democracies
Are At Their Strongest When
Individuals Feel They Are
Not only Encouraged,
But Obliged to
Participate
As Their
Voices
Really
Do
Count.
Conversely,
They Are Weakest
When Their Citizens Succumb to
Feeling that They Are Powerless, Insignificant,
Even Irrelevant, When They Are Led to Believe Nothing
They Do Will Have Any Impact on the Powers That Be, For
They Are Outsiders Who Are Only Able to Look In, That The
Truth of the Matter is Governmental Structures are Mere
Window Dressings Designed to Create the Illusion of Power
When, in Truth People Are but as Tiny Leaves Caught up &
Swept Downstream in the Mighty Torrent Of History. And
Since There Isn't Anything We Can Do To Change
This, Why Bother Even Getting Involved?
To Refute This Lie, the Ongoing Challenge
Of Any Democracy Is To Protect It
From Those Who Would
Manipulate The
System For
Their Own
Selfish
Goals

Lions and Tigers and Bears, Oh My!

Even Dorothy knew who to fear; why don't we? In 1982, when Ronald Reagan borrowed a line from Leon Trotsky's 1917 speech and spoke of communism taking its rightful place on the "ash heap of history," we as a people celebrated victory in the Cold War and put communism and the fear of communists behind us. We bid it adieu and considered it to be little more than a spooky villain in the dust of our rear view mirror; but, was it really over? As fate would have it, just as we lassoed the mighty Russian Bear of Soviet era communism, we saw out of the corner of our eye a little, cute, cuddly Chinese Tiger cub that we couldn't resist picking up. The rest is playing out the way it so often does for owners of exotic animals. The once cute and innocent grows over time into the aggressive animal it was destined to become. Before those who adopted it can adjust, the nature of the relationship turns and the cute little cub becomes a four hundred pound killer.

How Russian Bears and
Chinese Tigers Differ

Yes, it is true that we put that big old Russian Bear in its place, but as contests go, that wasn't anything compared to the potential challenge before us. While bears, by nature, are large and ferocious, they are also terribly awkward and clumsy. They have an unsteady gait and often roll over when attempting to sit up straight. They get pudgy and bloated with fat from laziness (just look at Winnie the Pooh), while tigers, on the other hand, are sleek and immaculately clean.

Tigers move silently through the forest, surefooted and careful to slouch down, waiting for the opportune moment to strike. They have no need to show forth their intentions or demonstrate force, for they are the consummate hunters. They know the value of sitting motionless, biding their time, waiting with uncommon focus for just the right moment to pounce. While bears often take on other bears in a demonstration of their strength, tigers have no need for such displays of force. They rarely make a premature stand, show their teeth or raise their voices. They prefer to sit quietly by and wait and wait for the perfect opportunity to strike. There is a reason most will hunt bears and avoid tigers.

I had a cat when I had a basement apartment in New York City. My home was in the back of the building, immediately next to the laundry room and the trash room, a true Shangri La for the urban mouse. I had often heard that New York had more rodents than people, but never thought too much about it until I got this cat. I also had a dog. He was into everything and then some, but not this cat. It just sat there hour after hour, day after day, staring at the baseboard.

Many a morning, I'd come out of my room and there would be the kill from the night before. There never was any chance of the cat losing the fight, just a dead mouse, lying lifeless on the carpet. Though only a house cat, and a declawed one at that, I learned that a cat, any size cat, never looks very threatening. They don't bark like a dog or prowl around like a bear. In fact, they appear totally disinterested as they lounge around preening themselves, looking totally non-threatening.

Many a wildebeest or zebra come to the water for a drink. They see the mighty tiger sitting on the rock as he normally does, enjoying the sun. This day, the tiger appears no more antagonistic than on any of the countless days before. Concerned, but thirsty, the unsuspecting victim bends his neck forward for a drink, a nice cool drink of refreshing water. Then, without notice, the tiger is suddenly upon him. There's never any question as to who will win for the tiger knows the value of biding his time. Day after day, he just sat there, totally at ease, until his prey became whittled down to complete complacency. Then, when everything was in the cat's favor, the attack occurred. There was no real competition to speak of, only a futile last ditch effort at defense, but never really a contest. It was too late for that. The patient tiger had carefully scoped out the situation and as a result, emerged once more victorious.

Please, Do Not Feed the Tiger

I want to be clear. I harbor no ill will toward the people of China. It is only the pernicious leadership that I fault. Indeed, I am a bit like those who admire tigers at the zoo, ever mindful that less than 1% of the total animal is problematic with its killer instinct. If that wasn't present, my home and my yard would be full of the beautiful creatures. Yet, that isn't the case. It is only because all of the rest of the animal is subject to and responsive to the directing of the head that I have no choice but to keep my distance and respect the sign saying, "Please, Do Not Feed the Tiger."

How It Will All Go Down
If We Don't Now Rise Up

What we need to come to terms with is the simple fact that the fall of nations is like the collapse of companies. In an effort to hold onto the confidence of all involved, companies will go to great lengths to hide their financial woes lest stocks and credit ratings plummet. Things look as normal as they can possibly make them right up until the last moment. Then, one fine morning, the plug is pulled and the whole thing collapses like an inflatable building that has just shut off the fans.

We Are In an Epic Struggle
Of
Freedom vs.
Tyranny
~ If Only We Could
Accept It ~

Clearly, It's Time to Talk about China

Nations the world over have consistently been able to turn to the United States, the birthplace of modern democracy, whenever their most basic human freedoms have been threatened. We have been the global power that has fought back and curtailed the authoritarian rule of the Hitlers, Mussolinis, Mao's, Stalins and Khrushchevs of the world. To now let down our guard and slowly, but oh, so steadily, hand over the role of dominant global power to a communist country that forbids the distribution of Bibles and routinely tramples the most basic of human rights just so we can profit off their cheap labor is the height of moral failures.

The Real Battlefield Is Ultimately Economic

We think we are safe because of our enormous military, but this is misguided. The truth of the matter is regardless of its size, it can't save us if we don't have the capital necessary to hold it up. The Soviet Union was strong right up to the last minute. Then, in the blinking of an eye, their economy collapsed. Almost immediately thereafter, their military unraveled and their once proud fleet of nuclear submarines and surface ships, which until recently patrolled much of the earth, suddenly lay abandoned, rusting in Soviet ports. When there are calls for enlarging our current global military presence to stand up to the growing threat of China, it is clear that Washington doesn't get it. We can't maintain a global military presence without the income to support it.

China understands this. That is why, learning from the mistakes of the Soviet Union, they have put the actual arming of the country last and instead have focused all of their efforts on first growing strong as a nation. Once this threshold is met, watch out. Their militarization will be fast and furious and will come just about the time the US will be too depleted, too gaunt, and financially anemic to respond.

Unlike the former Soviet Union where they were always on the field militarily, always advancing here and there, the Chinese are like the prize fighter who knows the very last thing a contender does is put on the gloves. This has lured us into believing we have nothing at all to worry about. So, we keep diverting our wealth to them by shopping at Wal-Mart while they are busy using this money to condition themselves and get into shape. Once they feel fully prepared to take us on, then, God forbid, we will be like the 90 pound weakling trying to defend ourselves against the ultimate of muscular opponents.

Excuse me for a moment.
I need to make a phone call ...

"Hello, National Archives?
Dig up Paul Revere's horse..."

The Chinese
Are Coming!

I'd Argue That Time
Is of The Essence

It is simply beyond my capacity to fathom the fact that to date no one on Capitol Hill has even mentioned the possibility of standing up to the Chinese. Isn't it obvious that if we continue down our current path of business as usual, in another four years chances are good that two things will have taken place? First, as mentioned, China will have siphoned enough wealth that we won't have any consumer strength left. It will all be in their pockets. This feeds into the second probability that this money will then go into China's military industrial complex, and we will be forced to spend whatever we have left on defense. That, however, will be a losing proposition as without any real tangible income from industry, we will only have the option to borrow. The problem, of course, is that we cannot borrow from Europe as they, too, are in the soup with us. The only nation with the capital to lend us money will be China, and I tend to doubt that they will be willing to fund our military defense.

Import Duties Aimed Specifically at China Are Our Only Hope

They will immediately bring our jobs back home, erase our trade deficit, restore our local, state and federal treasuries and deflate China's growing military threat before it is too late. We need to immediately place, across the board, graduated duties on all Chinese imports. Our goal is not to inflict damage on China. We need to be real clear about that. Rather, it is purely defensive; to protect ourselves from the unfair trade policies they have had in place for decades.

Few would argue that when someone is playing dirty, it is not only right, but morally responsible to take protective measures to defend against unfair assault. In light of this basic human right of self-preservation, the gradual but real introduction of import duties is warranted. I'd suggest a 25% increase per year for four consecutive years until we reach the level we have in mind. Quite simply, I am suggesting that we do this to bring home the very factories that have impoverished us with their departure and made China rich. It's as simple as that, for factories produce goods, and it is the sale of these goods that creates wealth.

Cut off the economic incentives to manufacture goods over there and in short order we will once again start producing our own consumer goods right here at home. Even if we lose trade with them, we are better off without it as they have tilted the whole equation in their favor. For the entire thing has been set up to drain the lifeblood out of our nation, and we are all suffering a dramatic loss in our standard of living because of it. Figure it out. It's not that complicated.

"But, We Don't Want To Set Off A Trade War!"

I hate to be the bearer of bad news, but anytime you live in a country where consumers are hard pressed to find any, and I repeat, *any* domestically made products, where virtually all of the merchandise on the store shelves have a "made somewhere else" label on them, there is little chance of an impending trade war. Why? Because it has already come and gone, and you've undoubtedly lost!

Let me tell you something else. . . the only thing more humiliating than being the wealthiest power on earth to lose to what started out as the poorest is to have a government so inept that it virtually slept right through it. Now that's humiliating. And yet, these same "leaders" have no shame. They now seek our vote to return them to office. Are they serious?! To now stir up fear among us over a potential trade war with China is like advising the Confederacy not to get on the wrong side of the North after Sherman returns from burning Atlanta.

Damn it!
We Shouldn't Have To Support
Communism Every Time We Shop.

Congress: Get busy and pass legislation aimed at restoring the very jobs that were rightfully here and never should have left our shores in the first place. Until this step is taken, our wealth will keep flowing overseas.

Quite simply, we need to listen to our vocabulary, to the words that flow from our lips. For there is indeed a reason we refer to factories as "plants." They, too, are like a farmer's field that takes the rawest of materials and blends them together in a unique and wonderful way so as to produce something entirely new that others crave and are willing to purchase. It's true. Just as a farm takes the raw materials of soil, sunlight, seed, water and air to create food, so, too, manufacturing plants take metals, glass, rubber and synthetics to create a whole host of products from automobiles and toaster ovens to electronics.

So quickly we forget that the American Revolution was fought over the right to manufacture.

Why? Why was the right to have our own factories so important? It is because our founding fathers realized something we have somehow forgotten, namely that the ground floor of economic prosperity is production. It is only after we create wealth by bringing to the table something entirely new that didn't exist before that we have something to trade. That position of affluence stays with us until we spend it down and have to go out and produce more. Like people, when nations sell stuff, they gain wealth and when they buy stuff they lose wealth.

An Economy is Like a Farm

In the final analysis, it doesn't matter or make the slightest bit of difference how many hours a farmer works or how nice the place looks. The barns can be nice and tidy, freshly painted and immaculately maintained. The tractors can be kept in tip-top shape, the fences mended and the house without blemish, yet none of this determines the health of the farm. All that matters is the size of the crop.

It's just that simple. That is why creating the "busy work" of paving roads and planting trees doesn't offset the money we are sending China every time we shop. They are the ones producing things and we are not. Instead, we are buying what they produce. Then, as if to add insult to injury, we are borrowing from them to prop up the economy we decimated by exporting our industrial base to them.

How You Know if Your Hometown and/or Country is in Trouble

Take a look around. Don't be fooled by employment numbers, for employment numbers alone can be misleading. A lot of people can be working, but if their labors are not in production, then you are not in a prosperous community. This simple point is something a huge number of politicians, and I dare say economists, don't get, but that's O.K. Sometimes it is up to simpletons like us to point out the obvious to those who we'd hope would know better, but unfortunately don't.

Now, hang in there with me and let's see if we can turn this thing around. O.K., by definition, prosperity is about increase and increase is about creating things that did not exist before. When we write a new song or grow a new crop or produce a new manufactured item that is of value to others and can be sold to others, then we are moving forward or "getting ahead." That's wonderful.

What we don't want is to be in an economic situation like the one I currently see in my community and perhaps the one you see in yours. All of the manufacturing jobs are gone. *Poof* they've disappeared. In their place there have sprung up all kinds of resale shops. In a town of roughly 30,000 people, there are now between 10 to 12 secondhand resale stores. It's pitiful. The once great economic powerhouse, the mighty United States of America, is no longer forging ahead, but now is sitting there, dead in the water, idle. Not only aren't we producing anything, we're just standing still like a cow chewing its cud, reprocessing that which we have already consumed. Increasingly, the only new products on the shelves are made overseas. My God! What has happened to the once proud, robust country I grew up in?

***Why not have a 20% rise in employment
instead of the measly 1 or 2%
we now experience?***

It's just as easy as it is ethical to accomplish. Just replace the "Made in China" labels with our old "Made in America" labels and we'll enjoy the same prosperity that was ours before our elected officials and selfish business executives opted to give it away to a nation that is using and will continue to use the proceeds to fund our demise.

The same production jobs that made China's economy soar can be ours once again by simply re-creating an environment where it makes good economic sense for Americans to manufacture the products that we Americans consume.

With a simple vote in Congress and stroke of the Presidential pen, we can make it more attractive to produce our own goods right here at home by putting import duties on Chinese goods. This will make Chinese goods more expensive than the goods made here in the USA, thus returning to us the home turf advantage. It will also level the playing field so as to offset four decades of China's artificially manipulating the whole equation in their favor.

If the people with whom I did business were shoplifting while they were billing me, you'd better believe I wouldn't just cut them a check.

No, of course not! I'd call the police and make darn sure there were some serious consequences for the theft. I would then calculate the cost of what was stolen and deduct it from the bill. If we did just that and included not only the cost of what was stolen from our government such as defense technologies, but also all of the cost due to American companies from theft of their intellectual property, loss of royalties and the loss of sales from boatloads upon boatloads upon boatloads of shipping containers filled with pirated materials (while this anemic government sat by and did absolutely nothing to stop it), then added penalties and interest (hey, the IRS and Courts do it all of the time), I think that supposed debt we owe them could be reduced to practically nothing. In fact, they might be the ones owing us.

Renegotiate Our Supposed Debt Already!

Each one of the advanced systems they got from us came at enormous cost to taxpayers. How many launches, for example, did it take to put a man on the moon and return him safely to Earth? I'll tell you. It took all of the Mercury, Gemini and then Apollo missions and before that there were years of test flights by pilots such as Chuck Yeager who laid the groundwork for rocketry.

Now, thanks to us, the Chinese will apply all of that research and experimentation to build their first and only spaceship. It will undoubtedly reach the Moon on their first try, thanks to all they got from our years of development. Then they, like the Japanese before them with the transistor, will claim all of the glory and use that knowledge in direct competition with us. Renegotiate our supposed debt already! To go from rice paddies to space in 40 years is utterly impossible. We owe them? Yeah, right, sure we do!

America's Dunkirk

If we had some real leadership in Washington, we'd recognize that there's all kinds of capital lying around. I believe people would love to extend it to us, with interest, if it was explained to them that it is an issue of national importance; that we have to change course now and in order to do this, we have to keep things going at home in the meantime. OK, that's an easy sale. Most Americans are already there in their thinking. All we have to do is explain how they can help.

I'd either instigate new financial vehicles or reinvigorate existing ones such as US Savings Bonds and enlist celebrities and other folks to encourage people to invest. I'd make the interest rates quite generous, non-transferable and available only to American citizens. I'd also make the payoff years down the road as has always been the practice with Savings Bonds. Do this, and we'll have people take to their savings like the British to their boats when they saved their troops at Dunkirk.

This is infinitesimally less expensive than borrowing from a foreign nation that has made it abundantly clear that any money coming to them from us will be used to fund a government hell bent on doing us wrong. For in the latter case, we not only have to repay the debt, we also have to fund additional defensive measures we will have to take to protect us from the monster we are creating.

Why Are We Funding Another Evil Empire?

While we're at it, I think it worthwhile to discuss having a Constitutional Amendment prohibiting the sale of Treasury Bills to foreign nations lest we get into this vulnerable position ever again. It is bad enough that we have allowed ourselves to become indebted, but to know that a sizeable chunk of our GNP goes directly into funding a military industrial complex out to harm us is absurd.

Then There Is Europe

Our allies in Europe and their currency, the Euro, are on the brink of financial collapse. Import duties on Chinese goods will have the additional benefit of supporting these democracies who now find themselves in desperate straits with massive unemployment, in large part, because of our trade policies that have reached beyond our borders to impact their economies as well.

The fix is not sending more aid to these countries nor is it printing more US currency to do so. The solution is to immediately pass significant trade legislation that will make it just as unattractive to produce goods in communist China as it is attractive to produce them right here in the democratic United States and democratic Europe.

Upset The Chinese?
They Hold Our Treasury Bills!

As newcomers to capitalism, China needs to know the other side of the equation. Firstly, there is some truth to the old adage that if a person owes the bank $1,000, the bank owns them, but if a person owes the bank $10,000,000, then they own the bank. They also need to know that there are no debtor's prisons in capitalism and declaring bankruptcy, while never easy, is always an option. Just because something is owed doesn't mean it should be repaid, especially if the lender is going to use the proceeds to harm the borrower. This truth applies to nations as well as neighbors.

Think about it, if England in the 1930's owed Germany billions of dollars prior to the outbreak of hostilities, do you think they'd be rushing to repay it? Of course, they wouldn't! If anything, they'd use their indebtedness as a bargaining chip to convince Germany to back away from its increasingly aggressive behaviors. Churchill was able to see the conflict in Europe long before his own people did. Likewise, Roosevelt was able to see danger long before the rest of America did. Both took steps to sound the alarm and prepare. Who in our national leadership is able to see the obvious and act?

The Only Reason
Not To Install Import Duties
Is Fear

When I share my proposal of starting graduated import duties against China, the overwhelming response I get is based on fear. What will they do? The fact is, China may have our promissory notes, but who has the power there? They are at the mercy of our good intentions to pay them off. History is replete with instances where well intentioned promises are never kept. History also tells us that decisions based on fear and desires to appease are by far the worst possible courses of action for a nation to take. If we are fearful of China's long term intentions, then we had better examine our fears now so can take preemptive steps to protect ourselves.

I am reminded of the wealthy couple (true story) who hired a skipper to handle their yacht. Their friends remembered that before the couple turned up missing, they had verbalized concerns about their new employee and often spoke of just how uncomfortable they felt whenever they were around him. Despite this, they lacked the inner strength and backbone to take control of the situation and fire him. Why? Because they feared what he might do if they upset him. Hoping things would improve if they didn't "rock the boat," they reluctantly went ahead and set sail on their long planned ocean voyage. Well, guess what? Neither they nor their yacht were ever seen again.

Shame on Us!
The Saddest Day
In American History

Some would consider the outbreak of the Civil War, the day we were viciously attacked at Pearl Harbor or the events of 911 as the saddest days in American history. I beg to differ. Tragic as they were, they were attacks brought to bear by others on the sovereignty of the United States. In time, each of those incursions was reversed and America emerged victorious with its core values.

No, none of them were the saddest day in American history. The saddest, in my estimation, occurred on the day that we, as the most powerful nation in the world, stood silently by and did absolutely nothing to prevent the horrific, ruthless slaughter of innocent civilians in Tiananmen Square. What was their crime? They were so audacious as to seek freedom of assembly, the right to vote and the right of self-determination. They looked to America to assist in their quest, even going so far as to erect a replica of the Statue of Liberty in their midst and we didn't so much as lift a finger to help. Nothing, nothing at all was done. No military threats were uttered, no troops repositioned, no sanctions taken. Why? It was because we didn't want to upset the Chinese communist regime and jeopardize the potential fortunes that American corporations were beginning to reap there.

On that day, America surrendered its soul. It sold it for a mess of pottage. Decades later, those who were not killed in the attack in Tiananmen Square still languish in China's prisons. Where's our sack cloth? Where are our ashes? Are the spirits within us so dead that even now we cannot even feel, let alone own, the shame that should confront and confound us?

With One Vote for Import Duties on China:

1) America will start to recover its industrial base.

2) We'll have the tax revenues for infrastructure.

3) The USA will become prosperous once again.

4) Parents will be home raising their kids instead of working two or more jobs just to pay the bills.

5) China will be forced to deal with internal pressures that will divert their resources away from its aggressive posturing.

LIST OF HEADINGS